START-UP ENGLISH BIOGRAPHIES

ROALD DAHL

Chris Powling

Evans

Evans Brothers Limited

Published by Evans Brothers Limited
2A Portman Mansions
Chiltern Street
London W1U 6NR

© in this edition Evans Brothers Limited 2009

Printed in China

Editor: Bryony Jones
Designer: Mark Holt

British Library Cataloguing in Publication Data

Powling, Chris.
    Roald Dahl. – (Start-up English. Biographies)
    1. Dahl, Roald – Juvenile literature. 2. Novelists, English –
    20th century – Biography – Juvenile literature.
    I. Title II. Series
    823.9'14-dc22

ISBN-13: 9780237539016

Picture acknowledgements: Cover (main) © Dahl Estate (top left) Jan Baldwin; **page 4** © Dahl Estate; **page 5** Jan Baldwin; **page 6 and 7** © Bremner & Orr Design Consultants Ltd 1996; **page 8** © Dahl Estate; **page 9 and 10** © Dahl Estate/Martyn F. Chillmaid; **page 11** © Dahl Estate; **page 12** © Dahl Estate/Martyn F. Chillmaid; **page 13** (left) Jan Baldwin (right) © Dahl Estate/Martyn F. Chillmaid; **page 14** © Dahl Estate; **page 15** Leonard McComb/Martyn F. Chillmaid © Life Magazine; **page 17** © Dahl Estate/Martyn F. Chillmaid; **page 18** © Dahl Estate; **page 19** Jan Baldwin; **page 20** Sanjiro Minimaikawa/Martyn F. Chillmaid; **page 21** © Dahl Estate/Martyn F. Chillmaid

VISIT OUR WEBSITE
Evans
www.evansbooks.co.uk

Contents

Who was Roald Dahl?

Have you heard of Charlie and the Chocolate Factory? Or read about George's Marvellous Medicine?

If your answer is yes, you're probably a fan of Roald Dahl already. If it's no, don't worry – you're in for a treat!

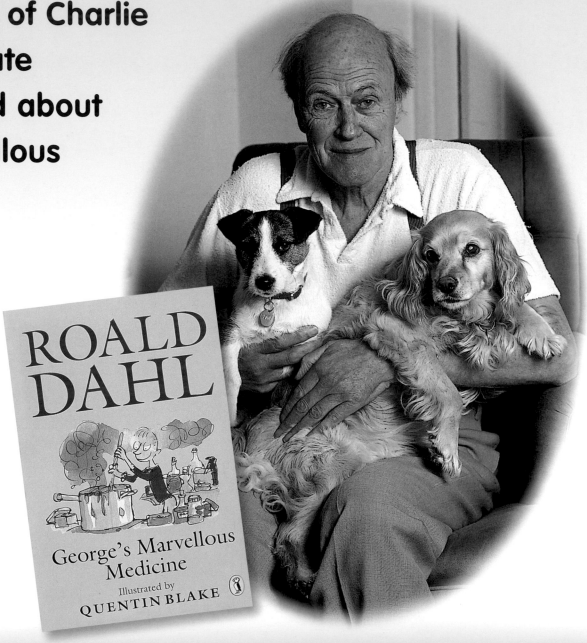

Factory   Medicine   fan

Roald Dahl was one of the most successful writers for children who has ever lived. He wrote his stories in a shed in his garden.

This is the story of his life.

successful

Million-selling stories

Roald Dahl died in 1990, but today he is still as popular as when he was alive. He wrote 18 books of stories and rhymes which have sold millions of copies all over the world. There is a special Roald Dahl museum that you can visit. It's lots of fun!

rhymes   museum

Roald Dahl's stories have been made into films, such as 'Matilda' and 'James and the Giant Peach'.

Life at home and school

Roald was born in 1916 in Cardiff, in Wales. His father died four years later, so Roald was brought up by his mother, who was Norwegian.

▶ Roald's father, Harald

▲ Roald and his mother

Norwegian

Roald loved living at home. When he went to boarding school, he was less happy.

▲ Roald Dahl took these photographs at his boarding school.

boarding school

Work and war

As soon as he could leave school, Roald travelled to Africa to seek his fortune. He spent two exciting years there working for the Shell Oil Company.

◀ Roald in Africa

In 1939 Britain's war with Germany began. Roald joined the Royal Air Force as a pilot.

fortune   Royal Air Force   pilot

◀ A painting of Roald wearing his pilot's uniform

Being a pilot was exciting, but very dangerous. Roald had a bad crash and his injuries made him limp for the rest of his life.

injuries   limp

Adventures in America

After this Roald was sent to America as a kind of spy. He published a story in a famous magazine about his adventures as a pilot. Soon he was writing more stories – including one called 'The Gremlins'. Walt Disney wanted to make the story into a film. He invited Roald to Hollywood.

▶ Roald with Walt Disney and the Gremlins

spy   published

Roald married an American film star called Patricia Neal. They had five children – Olivia, Tessa, Theo, Ophelia and Lucy.

▲ Roald and Patricia

◀ Gipsy House, where the Dahl family lived.

Disaster strikes

When Theo was a baby, in New York, his pram was hit by a taxi. Theo's brain was badly damaged. To help Theo and other children, Roald, a doctor and an aeroplane **modeller** invented a special type of **valve**.

▶ Theo Dahl as a young child

14

modeller   **valve**

The valve was called the Wade-Dahl-Till valve after the people who invented it.

Luckily, Theo got better by himself, but the valve saved the lives of thousands of children.

► Roald Dahl with Theo and young friends

Terrible troubles

Later, something worse happened. Roald's daughter Olivia died from a very rare kind of measles. Roald's book 'The BFG' has a special dedication to Olivia.

rare   measles   dedication

The Dahl family's troubles were not over. Roald's wife Patricia had a serious illness called a stroke. Roald organised a team of friends and neighbours to help her recover.

▲ **Patricia with Olivia and Tessa**

stroke

A shed full of stories

Amazingly, while all this was going on, Roald was becoming more and more successful as a children's author.

▲ He wrote his stories in this shed in his garden.

author

He sat in an old armchair with a wooden board propped across it. Then he would sharpen six yellow pencils and write on a pad of yellow paper.

▲ Inside Roald's shed

Roald once said, 'One of the nice things about being a writer is that all you need is what you've got in your head and a pencil and a bit of paper.'

Rich and famous

From Roald's head came books such as 'The Twits', 'Esio Trot', and 'The Giraffe and the Pelly and Me'. These books and others made him one of the richest and most famous writers for children there has ever been.

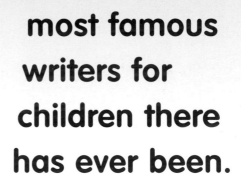

◀ He was a champion orchid grower too!

orchid

In 1983 Roald won a big prize for 'The BFG'. This book has pictures by Quentin Blake. He based the drawings for the Big Friendly Giant on Roald himself.

◀ Quentin Blake and Roald at work at Gipsy House.

After Roald died, his second wife, Felicity, set up the Roald Dahl Foundation. This charity helps children and adults with serious illnesses and problems.

Foundation   charity

Further information for

Key words introduced in the text

author	fan	measles	orchid	Royal Air Force
boarding school	fortune	medicine	pilot	spy
charity	foundation	modeller	published	stroke
dedication	injuries	museum	rare	successful
factory	limp	Norwegian	rhymes	valve

Background Information

Pages 6 and 7

The Roald Dahl Museum and Story Centre is in Great Missenden, Buckinghamshire.
Visit www.roalddahlmuseum.org for more information.

Pages 8 and 9

Roald tells us about his own life in his two books, "Boy" and "Going Solo". It is clear from these two books that he was always a bit of an outsider – someone who never quite behaved in the way people expected. Perhaps he took after his father. Harald lost his arm as a young man when he fell off a roof. Later he ran away twice to seek his fortune.

Pages 14 and 15

Theo developed a condition called water on the brain after he was hit by the taxi. The treatment that was used at the time included machinery that could often jam. Roald Dahl worked with his friend, Stanley Wade, who he knew through their shared hobby of flying model aircraft, to develop a valve which did not jam. Wade was a hydraulic engineer, and with the aid of the neurosurgeon Kenneth Till, he and Dahl successfully created this new technology, which helped thousands of children.

Pages 20 and 21

Roald loved being famous. He once said, 'I suppose I could knock at the door of any house where there was a child – whether it was in the US, Britain, Holland, Germany, France – and say "My car's run out of petrol; could you please give me a cup of tea?" And they would know me. That does make me feel good!'

The Roald Dahl Foundation helps children and families with brain and blood problems. Find out more at www.roalddahlfoundation.org.

Parents and Teachers

Topics for discussion

Discuss your favourite Roald Dahl books, giving reasons.

Why do you think Roald's books have become so famous?

Why do you think Roald's family set up the Roald Dahl Foundation after he died?

Suggested activities

Ask the children to write and illustrate a review of one of Roald Dahl's books.

Listen to an interview with Roald Dahl himself, and see more photos of him at www.roalddahl.com. Click on the Roald Dahl link.

Recommended resources

Boy: Tales of Childhood, Roald Dahl, Puffin, 2008

Going Solo, Roald Dahl, Puffin, 2008

www.roalddahl.com

www.roalddahlmuseum.org

www.bbc.co.uk/bbcfour/audiointerviews/profilepages/dahlr1. shtml

www.roalddahlday.info

Important dates

1916	Roald Dahl is born
1925	He begins at St Peter's Prep School, Weston-super-Mare
1930	He goes to Repton School
1938	Roald arrives in Africa
1939	He joins the RAF
1941	His injuries stop him flying
1942	Roald's first story 'A Piece of Cake' is published in America
1942-61	He writes short stories for adults
1961	He publishes 'James and the Giant Peach', his first children's book
1964	'Charlie and the Chocolate Factory' is published
1967	He scripts the James Bond movie 'You Only Live Twice'
1983	He wins the Children's Book Award for 'The BFG'; he wins the Whitbread Award for 'The Witches'; he divorces Patricia Neal and marries Felicity d'Abreu
1989	He wins the Children's Book Award for 'Matilda'
1990	Roald Dahl dies